T0198891

# Lessons On Leadership Learned in Grandpap's Garden

By Robert L. Furman

To order additional copies of this book, contact:
Xlibris
844-714-8691
www.Xlibris.com
Orders@Xlibris.com

ISBN:      Softcover        978-1-4134-6312-5

Print information available on the last page

Rev. date: 10/07/2022

To the memory of my father, Louis Furman, who was fondly referred to as Grandpap by not only his family but by most everyone with whom he came in contact. His simplistic life and the pragmatic manner in which he approached most of life's problems served as an example for others to emulate. While not formally educated beyond the age of thirteen, he was the consummate leader and teacher. Grandpap's life optimized all of the lessons contained in this book. Leaders would be well served if they would embrace the sage advice given to them by Grandpap.

# Table of Contents

I grew up with the greatest of blessings-a good family. My mother and father were dynamic parents, devoted unwaveringly to their children. They complemented each other so well that my sister, brother, and I knew just what to look for in a lifelong mate.

When my son was born, we began to call my dad "Grandpap." The new name was a good fit as he always possessed that quality of simple, profound insight we frequently associate with the elderly. Of course, those of us on the inside knew that Mom was his coach in the lessons of life. The two of them had conversations on a level all of their own. To credit Grandpap with sole responsibility for the wisdom set forth on the following pages would be like thanking Wilbur Wright for the airplane.

Grandpap's genius was in application. We used to say that he had four children-my sister, brother, me and his garden. To Grandpap, the garden was a kind of laboratory from which he derived the larger principles of living and leading. My earliest memories are of picking strawberries under his guidance."Only pick the ones you would want to buy yourself," he would say. "Never compromise your standards."

From spring thaw to the first snowflake, Grandpap would take an hour every morning and two in the evening on the weekdays to "work the garden." On the weekends, Mom had to order him in the house for lunch and dinner.

Every green thumb knows the sanctity of a garden. It is a place of solace, patience, and generosity. Whereas Grandpap's harvest consisted of vegetables, fruits, herbs and flowers, mine consisted of the wisdom shared in this book.

As a teacher and school administrator for over 30 years, I've kept a list of Grandpap's "lessons" in an old picture frame on my office wall. When I began making presentations at leadership conferences, I developed the garden concept into a metaphor for sound management practices. I cannot recall how many hours I spent after those presentations discussing the metaphor with audience members. Had I kept a list of all the transferable gardening wisdom they shared with me, you would be holding a masterpiece. Instead, I give you the original Grandpap-simple, sage, and still hanging on my wall.

# Lesson 1: Plants grow from the bottom up, not the top down.

It must have been after 9 a.m. when my mother woke me. She acted as though nothing was different, but we both knew he had let me sleep late. I dressed and had a warm breakfast before lacing my boots. Approaching the garden somewhat sheepishly, I nodded to Pap. In this fashion, I thanked him for the early morning relief.

I remember thinking that our garden was as large as a basketball court. Watering the plants took the good part of two hours. I held the nozzle of the hose in my hand and began showering the plants.

Grandpap never objected to my amateur methods; he simply steered me away from them. He raised his voice over the hose and said, "The bottoms are thirsty too! Plants grow from the bottom up, not the top down."

*"Leading consists of working with others as coach and mentor so that the organizational context in which improvement is valued and encouraged can be maximized by front-line workers."*
— *Edward Deming, 1994*

*"If you can work with people, and they participate in making significant decisions in your organization, you'll find there is much less resistance."*
— *Bernie Ebbers,*
*MCI WorldCom*

*"Company productivity is enhanced when departments view themselves as partners in progress and work together to maximize their potentials."*
— *Edward Deming, 1994*

*"No man will make a great leader who wants to do it all himself or get all the credit for doing it."*
— *Andrew Carnegie,*
*Industrialist*

The effective leader must approach the development and empowerment of his staff with the same passion that Grandpap approached the planting of his garden in early spring. Grandpap's passion was internalized by me and the others who helped him because he involved us from the grassroots. He shared with us his expertise then allowed us to do the job. It took a lot of hard work, but the rewards were many.

The effective leader realizes that to have a productive organization, he must inspire the use of all of the resources that are naturally embedded in his personnel.

Many leaders are reluctant to empower their staff. They lack confidence that their employees can make good decisions. Many leaders are power driven and enjoy the control that their position gives them. The notion of the hierarchical leader as the person "in charge" or "in control" is no longer functional. It is time to move to a new generation of leadership. This new leader can quite effectively be characterized as the gardener, creating the conditions for growth, planting ideas, talking with, listening to, nurturing and then sitting back and letting the natural talents and abilities of the workers come to the surface. This leadership style has been referred to in professional literature as "Servant Leadership." "At one level, the concept is an ideal, appealing to deeply held beliefs in the dignity and self-worth of all people and the democratic principle that a leader's power flows from those led. But it is also highly practical. It has been proven again and again that the only leader whom soldiers will reliably follow when their lives are on the line is the leader who is both competent and who soldiers believe is committed to their well-being"[1]. Grandpap made me feel that I could do the work and, consequently, I could.

[1]Kofman and Senge, 1995

## Lesson 2: Weeds must be removed from around the plant to enable proper growth.

As I watered one end of the garden, Grandpap weeded the other. It seemed that weeding was a daily chore, and Grandpap approached it with the spirit of a vigilante. It amazed me that even one day of neglect could lead to garden weeds. They seemed to grow faster than our plants. Grandpap had always said, "God's green earth wants to grow."

I turned off the water to help him with the grunt work. Kneeling down beside him, I asked why it was so important to remove the weeds. He lifted his head and surveyed the garden. Once he found the spot, Grandpap led me to the green pepper plants. "I haven't weeded the pepper row since last week," he said. "See how this one has a few yellow leaves? The weeds around it divert the sunlight and pollute the soil. Now, finding the weeds is only half the job. You've got to know how to pull 'em." I leaned over and ripped the weed away with a golf swing. Grandpap laughed and asked, "How do weeds grow?" It was a rhetorical question. I got down on my knees, dug my fingers into the dirt, and removed the bare stem of the weed by the roots. "From the bottom up," I laughed to myself.

> The effective leader identifies the weeds and systematically removes them from within the organization. He is data driven and takes decisive action when warranted.

*"You need to keep working in your job, team, business or organization while you also work on your job, team, business or organization. High performers develop the discipline to continually look at whether they're doing the right things in the best way."*

— Jim Clemmer,
Pathways to Performance:
A Guide to Transforming Yourself

*"The first role of holes: When you're in one, stop digging."*

— Molly Ivy, Columnist

*"One of the tests of leadership is the ability to recognize a problem before it becomes an emergency."*
— Arnold H. Glasow

*"The art of life lies in a constant readjustment to our surroundings."*

— Okakura Kakuzo

Like people, organizations can get sick and die. The effective leader has the innate ability to pick up obvious and not so obvious clues about conditions in the organization. He knows a weed when he sees one. Once a problem that threatens the organization is identified, he is persistent in overcoming the problem. The effective leader exhibits exceptional determination in solving problems and deflating negativity in the workplace. This is pivotal because U.S. companies lose about $3 billion a year to the effects of negativity, according to the Bureau of Labor Statistics.

Problems have a life span. All problems will eventually be solved or their impact neutralized. However, some problems like weeds never seem to go away. Problems that never seem to be solved have a way of draining the enthusiasm and motivation out of employees. These persistent problems are very much like the vines that grew in Grandpap's garden. On the surface you only see a small vine, but once you start pulling at it, you find that there is an extensive vine system just under the surface. You quickly realize that you are dealing with a much bigger vine than you first thought. The effective leader who directly deals with organizational problems may discover that what appeared as a minor problem is much more threatening to the organization than originally suspected. The effective leader must marshal all of the resources available to solve these habitual problems within the organization.

The effective leader does not sit back and wait for a problem to surface. He has systems in place to monitor the various operations in the organization and is data-driven. He has established employee teams that are charged with the responsibility of monitoring the various subsystems in the organization. These teams comprise of individuals who have a natural interest in dealing with numbers and data. To deal effectively with problems, the team needs to identify the size and scope of the problem in numerical terms. Once problems are identified, the effective leader calls on other employee teams to identify intervention strategies for solving the problems. Once interventions have been made and the problem appears to be resolved, the monitoring team continues to collect data to determine if in fact the problem has been eradicated. Like weeds, problems have a way of coming back when you least expect them. The effective leader needs to follow Grandpap's example and recognize that weeds need to be removed with regularity in order for growth to take place.

## Lesson 3: Symbiotic relationships exist between some plants.

Although Grandpap's garden was large by anyone's definition, he still was very aware of space limitations and made use of all available space. It was a routine practice for Grandpap to plant his pumpkins right next to his sweet corn. When asked why, he explained that it was a good use of space and that there was an added advantage of putting these two particular crops close together. When pumpkin plants are young, they require a great deal of sunlight. That is why they have a very broad leaf-to collect as much sunlight as possible. By contrast, corn grows much more slowly than pumpkins do and does not require as much sunlight in its early development, as evidenced by its very narrow leaf. As the two plants grow to maturity, the exact opposite needs arise. The mature pumpkin can be burnt by too much sunlight, whereas the corn needs strong sunlight to dry its husks and mature. In their mature state, the corn shields the pumpkins from direct sunlight, and the pumpkins at ground level do not interfere with the corn's need for ample sun.

Putting the two plants side by side in the field creates a strong symbiotic relationship, resulting in an efficient use of space and a better crop.

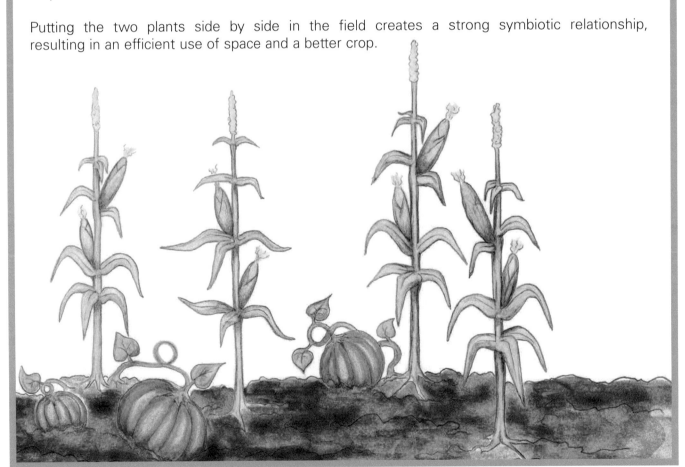

The knowledgeable leader understands that it is important to take into consideration the different skill and knowledge levels as well as attributes of his employees when hiring new personnel or assigning individuals to work teams.

*"Put one great teacher on every team. It will pull up the performance level of the entire team."*
— Joel Barker

*"Leadership should be born out of the understanding of the needs of those who would be affected by it."*
— Marian Anderson

*"An empowered organization is one in which individuals have the knowledge, skill, desire, and opportunity to personally succeed in a way that leads to collective organizational success."*
— Stephen R. Covey

Teamwork is the critical attribute of successful organizations. Employees want to be part of a winning team. Seeing teams meet with success is exciting, upbeat, and spreads a positive feeling throughout an organization. While not always possible to establish, the most successful teams seem to have a symbiotic relationship among its members. The effective leader assigns personnel to a team based on the unique skill level and attributes each employee possesses, being sure to have a comprehensive compliment of the skills and knowledge needed to achieve the team's goals. This diversity of skills and knowledge brings excitement and energy to the team, and each team member feels the team's synergy. The feeling that "as a team, we can do anything" permeates the work environment.

Establishing a team is not enough. It is critical for the leader to provide team members with an understanding of each member's unique skills and knowledge. Just as in Grandpap's garden, where the uniqueness of each plant was considered in the growth of the entire garden plot, leaders must build organizations considering the strengths and needs of the employees. When each team member understands the role he or she will play on a given project, little time is lost in getting to work. Also, it is critically important that each person knows how to be an effective team member. Time invested in team training is a critical step in ensuring successful team functions.

A vacancy in your organization presents the perfect opportunity to hire a person with the qualities, skills and attributes needed to supplement your team. The effective leader knows that the first step in the hiring process is writing an "ideal candidate" profile. Once this profile is written and the interview team is identified, a list of critical interview questions can be prepared. The next step is the actual interviews. In addition to looking for the skills and attributes you value in a candidate, you may also want to use some research-based criteria. The criteria published by Gallup, Imc., can be very helpful in discriminating among candidates. The Teacher Perceiver Interview Guide[2], for example, has ten theme areas around which I structure my interview questions. It is my understanding that Gallup, Inc. has research-based criteria for most professional positions.

Sometimes, team members become frustrated with their counterparts who have different attributes and orientations. When this happens, just as Grandpap took the time with me to explain how variation in the garden is critical, I have planned activities to show how important differences are in creating a strong organization. By engaging employees in activities that focus on personality types (sometimes as formal as using the Myers-Briggs Personality Inventory, sometimes less formal activities such as the North-South-East-West preference), the team members develop greater tolerance for and appreciation of each other.

[2]Available from Gallup Organization, Princeton, New Jersey

# Lesson 4: Some plants need extra support to continue to grow.

Grandpap had gone to the barn while I finished watering. I saw him return with a handful of stakes. "What's next?" I asked. "Tomato plants," he said. "They can't grow any higher without some support." I had noticed earlier in the morning how the tomato plants were beginning to sprawl over the garden. "You invite a whole kettle of problems when you grow tomatoes without supports," he said.

We planted the stakes and wrapped the tomato vines once around them. "These plants want to grow vertically. Just watch-in a few days, they will have taken to these stakes like birds to a tree."

The knowledgeable leader realizes that some of his followers, at certain times in their careers, will need special support to get through some particularly tough times. He sees to it that the necessary support programs and peer networks are in place for his followers.

*"Employee-centered leaders are sensitive to the needs and feelings of their people. They are supportive of employees, helpful to them, and concerned for their well-being."*

— F.A. Manske, Jr.
*Secrets of Effective Leadership*

*"Relationships that are durable and require frequent interactions provide incentives for people to assist and support one another."*

— Kouzes and Posner
*The Leadership Challenge*

*"A good objective of leadership is to help those who are doing poorly to do well and to help those who are doing well to do even better."*

— Jim Rohn

*"Some players you pat their butts, some players you kick their butts, some players you leave alone."*

— Pete Rose

Just like the stakes in Grandpap's garden, the effective leader understands that from time to time, some employees will need some extra support to get through particularly difficult times in their personal and/or professional lives. Employee Assistance Programs (EAPs) are an important component of workforce development and quality of worklife in organizational environments, providing the much-needed support to employees. EAPs were introduced in workplaces in the 1980's and became a mainstay of many organizations during the 1990's.

In our organization, we implemented a confidential EAP referral program for our employees during the 1990's. It comforts our employees to know that an experienced Employee Assistance Program counselor is only a phone call away. It is nick to know that there is someone who can help families respond to some of life's most common and stressful problems and that the use of this program is confidential.

As a leader, I have also made use of networking as an employee support strategy. I have worked at establishing networks of people who could provide support to their fellow employees with special needs. One key to being able to establish effective networks is getting to know your personnel on a personal level in order to make proper matches. Sometimes these personal networks have grown from the professional support networks I established pairing new hired novices with experienced mentors.

Investigations from a wide variety of disciplines consistently demonstrate that social support—the quality of interpersonal relationships—serves to enhance productivity, psychological well-being, and physical health. The California Department of Health, in its publication Friends can be Good Medicine, reports that social support not only enhances wellness but also buffers against disease, particularly during times of high stress.

## Lesson 5: Rotate the crops to eliminate soil depletion.

We always had a bare plot in the garden. That year, it was in the far west corner where the zucchini had grown the year before. Grandpap was very methodical about crop rotation.

"What'll you plant here next year?" I asked him. "Probably garlic. The soil is healthy and I've had little luck elsewhere with garlic," he said.

I learned from Grandpap that each crop uses the soil in a different way. If one type of plant is left in the same garden spot for too many years, the soil in that area becomes nutrient deficient.

> The knowledgeable leader, who empowers his followers through delegating work, understands that he must be careful not to overuse his naturally high productive followers or he will burn them out. He must rotate the work among his total staff.

*"People's sphere of influence ought to be over something relevant to the pressing concerns and core technology of the business."*

*— Kouzes and Posner*
*The Leadership Challenge*

*"Besides helping others, delegation is the key to the leader's sanity. You can't do it all by yourself. The more you try, the greater the pressure and tension."*

*— F.A. Manske, Jr.*
*Secrets of Effective Leadership*

*"Management is about arranging and telling. Leadership is about nurturing and enhancing."*
*— Tom Peters*

*"Support the strong, give courage to the timid, remind the indifferent, and warn the opposed."*
*— Whitney M. Young Jr.*

The knowledgeable leader seeks ways to increase choice and provide greater decision-making responsibility to his followers. These leaders understand the power of delegating work but at the same time realize that effective delegating requires a great deal of sensitivity to others. The knowledgeable leader understands that every follower's empowerment needs and abilities are different. They get to know what these varying levels of need and ability are and take this into consideration when assigning tasks. It is important to consider the delicate balance between the work needed to be done and worker morale. By rotating responsibilities, you will avoid the pitfall of boredom while allowing for training opportunities. It also allows you to have a backup plan in case one worker is unable to work or leaves the organization.

Like Grandpap in his garden, knowledgeable leaders are careful not to overburden the strong workers and burn them out. They rotate assignments and are sure to assign tasks that can result in success.

Two critical elements must be present to facilitate a successful practice of delegating. The first is mutual trust. The leader must trust that his followers are willing and capable of performing the assigned tasks. The second requirement is support. The leader must fully support his followers in their efforts to make decisions and perform various tasks. It is critical to give the followers all of the pertinent information they will need. When this delegation takes place, it is important that the followers understand their role. This can be accomplished by the leader communicating whether he expects the delegates to 1) support the decision he makes with no input, 2) study the problem and develop possible solutions, 3) work together with leader to brainstorm ideas and possible solutions with the understanding that the leader will make the final decision, 4) work together with leader until entire group reaches consensus or 5) work on problem with total autonomy to solve the problem. Leadership needs and expectations change depending on the circumstance, just as the garden soil needs change from year to year.

## Lesson 6: Some plants will not grow as quickly as others even though the conditions are the same.

There was a long-standing joke about garlic in our home. My mother would tease Pap that she could never make spaghetti sauce because the garlic supply was so unpredictable. Pap viewed her jests as a challenge and tried year after year to optimize the garlic harvest. The joke was that he never did. Garlic was the one plant he never completely understood.

I lifted my head from my work and asked the perennial question, "How's the garlic this year, Pap?" Earlier in the morning I had seen that the garlic was not growing uniformly. Some plants were healthy, while others seemed hopeless. "These plants have minds all their own," he said. "Each year they give a little, but I never know which ones will produce in any given year." I decided to join in on Mom's fun and said, "I'll ask Mom to buy some Ragu at the grocer's."

The knowledgeable leader understands that variation in the professional growth of employees, while all conditions appear to be the same, is often due to the degree to which each individual's personal needs are being met in the workplace. Understanding this, the knowledgeable leader takes the necessary steps to determine the needs of his employees and personalizes their professional growth opportunities accordingly.

*"There are as many ways to change and improve as there are people and organizations trying to do so."*
— Jim Clemmer

*"An individual will act in a certain way based on the expectations that the act will be followed by a given outcome and on the attractiveness of that outcome to the individual."*
— Victor Vroom
Work and Motivation

*"Specific goals increase performance, and difficult goals, when accepted, result in higher performance than easy goals."*
— J. Stacey Adams

*"Leadership is lifting a person's vision to higher sights, the raising of a person's performance to a higher standard."*
— Peter Drucker

The adage "You can lead a horse to water but you can't make him drink" is a good metaphor for this lesson. Even though a leader works to ensure that all employees are given the benefit of the same professional development activities, he must realize that some will reap great benefits from the experiences while others will gain little. This variation is the result of each individual's thirst for learning and his or her personal level of motivation. The "one size fits all" approach to professional development does not work. Just as Grandpap said about his garlic, employees too "have minds all their own."

David McClelland, in his book ,The Achieving Society, outlines the Three Needs Theory as including
1. Need for Achievement (personal responsibility, feedback, moderate risk)
2. Need for Power (influence, competition)
3. Need for Affiliation (acceptance, friendship, cooperation)

These three needs are common to all people but just as in Grandpap's garden, even though the environmental conditions are the same, employees will vary in what it takes to meet these needs. The maturity and perceptions of an individual will impact on their performance.

The order of importance of needs to the individual, as outlined by Abraham Maslow, begins with man's physiological needs of hunger, thirst, sleep, etc. When these needs are satisfied, they are replaced by safety needs. Next is the need for love or belonging, and to give and receive friendship.When these are satisfied, the esteem needs-i.e., the desire for self-esteem, self-respect, recognition and appreciation-follow. Finally, individuals have a need for self-actualization or a desire for self-fulfillment, which is an urge by individuals for self-development, creativity and job satisfaction. The knowledgeable leader takes time to consider the needs of her employees and takes steps to personalize the professional growth opportunities.

## Lesson 7: Don't ever think you are too good to get your hands dirty.

To Grandpap, gardening was exercise for the body and the soul. Although he was getting on in years, he never lost his work ethic.

It was nearly lunchtime and we were exhausted. Grandpap had one last project for me before going inside to eat. There was a pile of large rocks that he had been saving around the side of the house. I was to dig a shallow trench along the backside of the garden and fill it with the rocks. This would contain the soil during heavy rains.

With an overloaded wheelbarrow, I navigated precariously back across the yard and around the garden. I wanted to be finished by noon, so I set to digging the trench vigorously. Five minutes must have passed before I noticed that Grandpap was trenching from the other end. We finished in no time, and he was just as soon on his knees lodging the rocks into the dirt. We were done before Mom called us in for lunch.

The effective leader strives to develop followership as opposed to subordination. He understands that a key characteristic of a leader who promotes followership is his personal demonstration of followership. Effective leaders often work along side those they lead.

*"Leadership is practiced not so much in words as in attitude and in actions."*

— *Harold Geneen*

*"A real leader has the ability to motivate others to their highest level of achievement; then gives them the opportunity to and freedom to succeed."*

— *F. G. "Buck" Rogers*

In any organization, there are leaders and followers. However, in some organizations the leader creates an environment that perpetuates subordinates, not followers.

Subordinates do as they are told to do. They want marching orders. Subordinates provide a strong backbone to an organization. They get the work done as directed but do little else. They are not self-directed workers.

Followers are people committed to a vision of what the organization can become. They become the champions for the organization. They work aggressively to advance the organization because they feel an ownership to it mission, ideals and values.

The leader who promotes a followership culture needs to help his workers understand and embrace followership. One way to cultivate followership is to work along side your workers as Grandpap did, modeling how good followers work. This practice also reinforces the idea that followership culture is not restricted by rank or position. Everyone and anyone within the organization can pitch in and help a colleague with his or her work.

According to Robert Kelley in his book, The Power of Followership, there are four areas that leaders should address to help staff to become more effective in the followership role. 1. Help the organization define/redefine leadership and followership through open discussion. 2. Attend to the development of the specific skills needed to be an effective follower. 3. Review performance assessment and feedback documents and guidelines. 4. Collaborate to create organizational structures that encourage the taking of followership roles.

The effective leader knows that many individuals functioning within a followership environment grow into self-directed and committed workers. They make decisions on their own that are consistent with organizational goals, because the followers understand the mission of the organization and are emotionally committed to a set of ideas that support that mission.

## Lesson 8: If you want a straight furrow, focus on the end of the row, not your feet.

Having returned from lunch sufficiently rested, I was given the arduous task of creating a new furrow for additional potato plants. Planting furrows had never been my forte. The rows always came out looking more like mole tunnels than garden trenches.

Pap indicated where he wanted the furrow and I set to it with our trusty old manual plow. I took it nice and slowly, but after two yards, I began to veer. "There's a trick to this," Pap interjected. "To let you do it?" I half-joked, half-begged. "Close," he said, walking to the end of the row and anchoring a stake there. "Focus your eyes on this stake, not on your feet. Now give it another try."

I took his advice and plowed for about 20 yards without lifting my eyes from the stake. When I reached the end, I turned and saw the straightest furrow I have ever plowed. "Why haven't you shared this secret with me until now?" I asked him. But Grandpap hadn't heard, as he had already gone to the compost heap.

> **The knowledgeable leader knows the importance of keeping focused on the organization's mission. He also knows that it is his responsibility to put the stake in the ground.**

*"Successful people begin with the end in sight."*

— *Stephen Covey*
*Seven Habits of Highly*
*Successful People*

*"Visions are about possibilities, about desired futures. They're ideals, standards of excellence. As such, they're expressions of optimism and hope."*

— *Kouzes and Posner*
*The Leadership Challenge*

*"Effective managers live in the present—but concentrate on the future."*

— *James L. Hayes*

*"The very essence of leadership is that you have to have a vision."*

— *Theodore Hesburgh*

The shortest distance between two points is a straight line and the most time-efficient way to get from point A to point B is to follow that straight line. The knowledgeable leader must not look at his feet but must have a vision for the organization that is well out in front. The most valuable contributions the leader makes to the organization are the formulation, articulation, and constant indoctrination of the organization's mission. Once all parties understand the mission, it is the leader's responsibility to energize his employees to work in concert to achieve that mission.

John Naisbitt uses the term "alignment" to describe the common focus of a group of people toward a common goal. In its purest form, alignment occurs when everyone in the organization works unselfishly toward achieving its mission. The effective leader does everything in his power to maintain this alignment. The first and most critical step is to clearly articulate the organization's mission. Once all members of the organization know the mission, the leader must keep her followers focused and help those individuals with personal missions to blend their goals into the overall mission of the organization.

The knowledgeable leader understands the value of beginning with the end in mind. Just as Grandpap advised, it is necessary to set one's sights on the target at the end of the row, not on the steps taken to get there.

## Lesson 9: The soil must be prepared properly to have a productive harvest.

One of my favorite Grandpap-isms was "Soil is royal." He spent as much time preparing the soil as a scholar does researching his thesis. The compost heap in the side yard was no rose bush, but it guaranteed rich, healthy soil every year. Pap filled the wheelbarrow and pushed it beside the bare plot. I took a rake and spread the compost as he dumped it. It was moist and almost black in color.

Fertile soil is gold to a gardener. Pap knelt down and took a handful, letting it sift through his hands. "This will make a difference next year," he said. Two months later I found Grandpap planting garlic bulbs in that plot. They would have all winter to rest in that nutrient-rich ground.

Grandpap was nothing if not persistent.

## The effective leader creates an environment that provides for the social and emotional needs of his followers.

*"You've got to love your people more than your position."*
— *William James*

*"The deepest principle in human nature is the craving to be appreciated."*
— *F.A. Manske, Jr.*
*Secrets of Effective Leadership*

Grandpap knew the soil required proper preparation to become productive. Translating that to our organization, I have built programs on the assumption that a person's behavior is a function of his/her self-esteem, and that self-esteem results from a synthesis of experiences gained from interactions with those viewed as "significant others." In all organizational hierarchies, subordinates automatically view their leader as a significant other.

Almost all experiences impact upon a person's self-esteem in some way, but four intrinsic motivators of human behavior compel an individual to seek certain types of experiences from those viewed as significant in any organization. The effective leader understands these human needs and the role of being a significant other, and works to create an environment in which these needs are met.

The intrinsic needs of followers include:
1. A need to feel as though they belong and are connected to other individuals and groups within the organization.
2. A need to feel noticed, recognized, appreciated, and special to the organization.
3. A need to feel as though they have a degree of control over what happens to them in the organization.
4. A need to feel they have a clear understanding of what is expected of them, how the organization works, and the rules and policies that structure the organization.

The following are ideas that I have found successful.
· Establish a sense of community by promoting the establishment of traditions, i.e., annual breakfasts, holiday parties, end-of-work-week doughnuts, employee softball games, traditional ceremonies, and gifts for people leaving the organization.
· Establish an "open suggestion box" concept by placing a large piece of paper on a wall that everyone sees at some time during the day. Instruct your followers to anonymously list their problems and then deal with the problems during an open meeting. Brainstorm solutions and reach a consensus as to which solution will be tried. Direct the person who put the problem on the board to cross it off when the prob lem has been resolved. If it is still listed when the next meeting is scheduled, brainstorm a new solution. This develops a sense of joint ownership of the organization and gives you r followers a feeling of power.
· Invite visitors to your place of business. This is a golden opportunity to validate your employees. I always made it a point to ask my employees to share some of our exemplary practices with visitors.
· Be sure to have all rules, policies and practices clearly defined. Let your followers help identify the rules and practices. This fosters a strong sense of power as well as ownership in the organization.
· Be sure to recognize the special contributions of your workers. A small note of recognition goes a long way in satisfying an employee's need for recognition. Recognition in front of co-workers is even more powerful.

The knowledgeable leader understands that the soil of the organization is the environment and that behavior of persons cannot be changed, but circumstances in the environment can be arranged to bring out the best in each employee.

## Lesson 10: Plants die from the top down, not the bottom up.

One of Grandpap's patented teaching techniques was putting the student on the spot. He led me over to the carrot plants with that spirited glint in his eye. "Now, tell me which plants are dying." I knelt down and looked under the leaves of a few plants. I felt them to determine whether they were hardy. One was noticeably thin and withered with several brown leaves. "This one," I answered. "And?" Pap continued. I inspected several more to no avail. "Only one," I repeated.

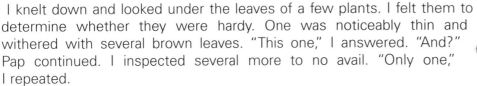

The glint in his eyes shone brighter for victory. "Signs of sickness in a plant may appear anywhere. You were wise to check the leaves and stems. But when a plant starts to die, it starts at the top. The one you identified is certainly dying, but there are others too." He pointed to one far more robust than my candidate. "Don't neglect this one," he said. "The leaves at the top are yellowish and desiccated. It's sick, to be sure, but it can be recuperated."

As a kind of plant doctor, Pap had a knack for early detection.

The effective leader understands that employees spend a lot of time watching what he does, and what they see sets the behavior standard for the organization. The leader's actions are noticed, commented upon, and eventually internalized by the organization so that the organization becomes a reflection of the person at the top. If the leader shows signs of weakening, the organization will start to weaken.

*"You have achieved excellence as a leader when people will follow you everywhere if only out of curiosity."*
*— Colin Powell*

*"When people respect someone as a person, they admire her. When they respect her as a friend, they love her. When they respect her as a leader, they follow her."*
*— John Maxwell*

*"People do not follow uncommitted leaders. Commitment can be displayed in a full range of matters to include the work hours you choose to maintain, how you work to improve your abilities, or what you do for your fellow workers at personal sacrifice."*
*— Stephen Gregg*

*"People don't at first follow worthy causes. They follow worthy leaders who promote worthy causes."*
*— John Maxwell*

Just like the plants in Grandpap's garden that show signs of decay, if a leader starts to loose enthusiasm, gets discouraged, or becomes overly negative, his followers will adopt these same characteristics. When this occurs, the organization starts its decline, and if leadership behavior continues in a negative direction, the organization will eventually reach a total state of ineffectiveness.

Even if a negative leader has a worthy message, it will fall on deaf ears. Every message that followers hear from their leader is filtered through their perceptions of that leader. Only if they consider his to be credible, of sound character, passionate about their vision and hopeful, will they then believe the message has value.

The effective leader should take time to periodically examine his behavior in the work place. Take the time to reflect on how your behavior is viewed by your followers. Are you practicing the Golden Rule? Are you treating others as you would like to be treated? When your followers look at you, do they see a person dedicated to his job? Do they see a person always doing his best work? Do they see a person who is strong, alive and growing professionally?

If you discover that you need some water and fertilizer at your roots, take the steps to get the nourishment you need. In some cases, you may find you need professional help to deal with some issues. Consider who and what refills the vessel that sustains you. Leadership is very demanding and draining. Be aware of signs of physical and mental strain. Take care of yourself. You and your organization need you to be well. Otherwise your sickness will spread to your organization just like the faltering tops of Grandpap's plants would eventually kill the plants if nothing were done to monitor them.

## Lesson 11: Flowers around the garden only add to its appearance.

Our garden made up in size and diversity for what it lacked in decoration. Grandpap had no interest in adornments. Other gardens in the neighborhood were lined with sunflowers and lilies. Ours was a model of pragmatism. "The quality of a garden is in the quality of its produce, period," Grandpap would say.

But there was a certain beauty to our garden, after all. The crops were planted in well-manicured lines. The soil was dark and weedless. And when the plants began to yield, the garden was fabulously colorful.

> While the master leader knows the importance of having his organization being positively viewed by potential patrons, he understands that all public relations efforts must accurately depict what is happening within the organization.

*"Opportunity is missed by most people because it is dressed in overalls and looks like work."*

— *Thomas Edison*

*"Well done is better than well said."*

— *Ben Franklin*

*"If success is not on your own time, if it looks good to the world but does not feel good in the heart, it is not success at all."*

— *Anna Quindlen*

*"Everything you do or say is public relations."*

— *Unknown*

Grandpap knew that the best marketing strategy was to be known for the straight-forward quality of the gardening produce. In kind, an effective leader should develop an organization that is known for being results-oriented.

Many people look at public relations initiatives as a deodorant covering up problems. The thought is that if these individuals were doing their jobs well, the public relations effort would be unnecessary. While this attitude that quality work results in a quality organization is desirable, this view overlooks one basic fact. Every organization has a public-relations program, formal or informal, that operates whenever their employees, services and products interface with their patrons.

In service fields, it is the person who comes in direct contact with the client who makes the most significant statement of public relations in his or her actions, courtesy, competence . My attitude is that all people within the organization must realize this macro nature of public relations. In addition, a quality organization should have a formal public relations program that accurately depicts the organization. Public relations is communicating and just as Grandpap advised, this initiative should be reflecting the quality of the organization, not distracting from it.

## Lesson 12: Harvest no crop before it is ready.

Every year, Grandpap would turn the strawberry harvesting responsibilities over to my neighborhood friends and me. He felt that strawberries were a good plant for beginning gardeners because they taught the importance of timing. In other words, every kid knows a ripe strawberry when he sees one.

One of the benefits of growing strawberries was that they ripened regularly and continuously throughout the summer months. In my neighborhood, all summer Sunday afternoons began with strawberry picking. I had the secret privilege of taking sneak peeks at the week's harvest on Saturdays.

It was mid-afternoon by now, and Grandpap was inside taking a break from the sun. I drifted toward the strawberry patch and was pleased with what I saw there. This was the one crop I knew well. I could categorize the berries into three categories just from a quick glance: 1) ready for tomorrow, 2) probably next week, and 3) at least two weeks. As master of the garden for that fleeting moment, I took it upon myself to evaluate the taste-potential of the largest ones.

**The effective leader recognizes that persons in the organization are ready for different leadership expectations at different times.**

" . . . much of the art of being a good teacher, healer or minister consists largely of staying just one step ahead of your patients, clients or pupils. If you are not ahead, it is not likely that you will be able to lead anywhere. But if you are two steps ahead you may lose them. If people are one step ahead of us, we usually admire them. If you are two steps ahead we usually think they are evil . . ."

— M. Scott Peck

"You have to recognize when the right place and right time fuse and take advantage of that opportunity."
— Ellen Metcalf

"Leadership and learning are indispensable to each other."

— John M. Kennedy

"Leadership involves finding a parade and getting in front of it."

— John Naisbitt

Just as there is an appropriate time for harvesting the crops, there is also an appropriate time to communicate information to staff members. Not all members of the staff are at the same level of readiness to accept new strategies and not all staff members have the same level of maturity for accepting supervisory feedback. Hersey and Blanchard's work with situational leadership can be very useful. The grid they have developed addresses the maturity level of the staff and the complexity of the task. Different approaches are used, depending on the situation and the individual.

Knowledgeable leaders know that adult learners need to be given information that is particularly connected with their experience. When involving employees in learning experiences that stretch them, keep in mind Dewey's concept of "experiential growth" and the notion of "learning from experience." For the adult learner, information becomes more relevant when it addresses their daily dilemmas, concerns and stages of professional development[4] and when it allows for adult learners to share these experiences with other colleagues in conversational frameworks that are both challenging and supportive. Although it often takes more time for the leader, offering a menu of topics scheduled at a variety of times allows employees to make choices based on their perceived needs and allows leaders the opportunity to recommend or require topics that would be most beneficial based on the readiness of the employee.

Knowledgeable leaders know that employees will be ready for different levels of responsibility and training at different times. Although the signs of employee readiness will not be as obvious as the strawberries in Grandpap's garden, the knowledgeable leader makes use of both informal impressions and supervisory reports to develop a continuum of growth experiences.

[4]Elbaz-Luwisch, 1997

31

## Lesson 13: Always give people more than they expect.

Grandpap's success as a gardener extended beyond the four walls of our home. The neighbors would stop by regularly to purchase produce at the neighborly price. The "Furman dozen" became known throughout the township as the best deal around.

That day it was Mrs. Bosco who came to make a purchase. She lived a few houses down and was one of our regular customers. Grandpap greeted her and handed me her basket. "What'll it be today, Susan?" he asked. She asked for green beans, peppers, yellow onions and carrots. I promptly filled the basket using the measure that was in each container and returned it to Grandpap. He inspected the contents and reached under the table where he kept the premier vegetables, then placed an extra handful of beans and peppers on top. He handed the basket to Mrs. Bosco.

Mrs. Bosco politely resisted at first, but Grandpap urged her to accept the extras. "It's the least we can do to express our gratitude, Susan."

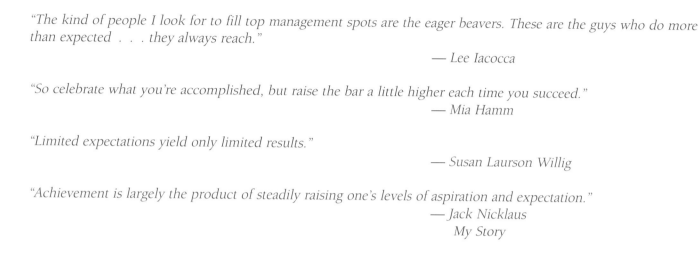

The effective leader creates an organization whose reputation is grounded in documented success and regularly exceeds established expectations. The bar is continually being raised through an element of surprise.

*"The kind of people I look for to fill top management spots are the eager beavers. These are the guys who do more than expected . . . they always reach."*

— Lee Iacocca

*"So celebrate what you're accomplished, but raise the bar a little higher each time you succeed."*

— Mia Hamm

*"Limited expectations yield only limited results."*

— Susan Laurson Willig

*"Achievement is largely the product of steadily raising one's levels of aspiration and expectation."*

— Jack Nicklaus
*My Story*

Overachievers are everywhere in organizations. They give more than is expected with some degree of regularity. This is a great asset to an organization when it is done in accordance with the goals of the organization and the effective leader recognizes the potential of "added value" and works with it.

Many organizations are committing performance standards to writing and the accompanying rating systems identify "exceeds expectations" as a viable rating category. In the Education field, where baseline test scores are identified for students, individual pupils and entire school districts are rewarded for exceeding expectations.

Travel brochures often boast that the accommodations or destination will exceed the expectations of the client. Just as Grandpap surprised his customers by giving them more produce than they expected, travelers are delighted to enter their hotel room to find a basket of fruit or special comforts beyond those included in the bill.

A simple way to impress people at a meeting can be accomplished by incorporating an element of surprise by providing food and drinks and small prizes. Their basic expectation of coming to learn will be embellished by practical ideas and take-aways that were a part of the presentation. They will leave with more than they expected and remember the meeting all the more for it just as Mrs. Bosco did with her extra produce.

## Lesson 14: Plants need a strong root structure in order to grow hardy and produce a good crop.

Mrs. Bosco had left and Grandpap was back at the soil. He had a habit of clearing the soil around the roots of a plant to inspect its health, and now he was tending to the red lettuce.

"Take a look here, Bob," he said, pointing at the ground around one plant. "The soil is loose and rich, and the lettuce loves it." He spread the dirt away with his hands and exposed the roots. "The roots have run deep and wide. That's one sign of a strong plant."

I knelt down and took a few gingerly tugs at the lettuce plant's roots. They were firm and thick. I felt a flash of insight coming on and said, "The roots are like the engine of a plant, aren't they?" "That's right," Pap said and added, "and the soil is the oil."

He paused, and at the same instant we both shouted, "Royal oil!" I suppose we were becoming a little delirious with all the hard work.

> The knowledgeable leader understands that the roots of the organization are embedded in the ethical and virtuous behavior of its leader.

*"People who had the greatest clarity about both personal and organizational values had the highest degree of commitment to the organization."*

*— C.C. Pinder*
*Work Motivation:*
*Theory, Issues and Applications*

*"People are changed, not by coercion or intimidation, but by example."*

*— F.B. Manske*
*Secrets of Effective Leadership*

*"Your position never gives you the right to command. It only imposes on you the duty of so living your life that others can receive your orders without being humiliated."*

*— Dag Hammarskjold*

*"My business is not to remake myself but make the absolute best of what God made."*

*— Robert Browning*

*"Set the course of your life by three stars—sincerity, courage and unselfishness. From these flow a host of other virtues . . . He who follows them will obtain the highest type of success, that which lies in the esteem of others."*

*— Dr. Monroe E. Duetsch*

The knowledgeable leader knows that his actions will speak more loudly than his words. How the leader treats the weakest link in the organization says more than awards and public messages. The leader's actions must complement the organization's goals and mission. As individuals, we are drawn to powerful, successful individuals and we tend to take on their behaviors.

Ethics is not the glamorous side of leadership, yet it is a critical ingredient for success. In fact, it is so important that it is hard to discuss leadership without interjecting the issue of ethics. It's pervasive, affecting the behavior of leaders in everything they do—making decisions, exercising judgements, etc. Ethical leadership is concerned with fairness, equity, commitment, responsibility and obligation.

The knowledgeable leader must be a model of ethical behavior. He should be governed by traditional ethical guidelines that are integrated with the values of a democratic society. These ethical guidelines include respect of all members of society, tolerance for divergent opinions and cultures, equality of persons, and equal distribution of resources. How well the leader adheres to these guidelines determines how deep the roots of the organization will run. The deeper the roots, the stronger the organization.

The roots of our belief systems become the foundation for our behaviors as leaders just as the roots of the plants were the foundation of Grandpap's garden. It is essential that we recognize that and develop the best of what God gave us.

## Lesson 15: Grandpap knew the importance of having the necessary tools and resources at hand.

It was now late in the afternoon. Clouds had moved in overhead, and I remembered that an evening storm was expected. Pap must have remembered too, because he walked to the backside of the garden to check on our newly dug trench. We had used arm strength to lodge the rocks into the ground, and I began to fear it was not enough. "How do you think they'll hold?" I asked him. "Depends on the rain," he said, scratching his chin.

I got an idea and slipped away into the barn. Grandpap's barn was a virtual museum of tools, new and old. That one barn had the resources to build anything from a soapbox derby car to a four-car garage. On any given weekend, he'd have tools lent out all over the neighborhood.

I grabbed two tamping bars and raced back to the garden. "Perfect choice!" Pap shouted. "We'd better hurry!"

## The knowledgeable leader understands that resources are not unlimited and are not always controllable.

*"Perhaps too much of everything is as bad as too little."*

— *Edna Ferber*

*"The first wealth is health."*

— *Ralph Waldo Emerson*

*"The guy with the most resources doesn't win. The guy who utilizes his resources best wins."*
— *Chuck Knight*

*"The greatest achievement of the human spirit is to live up to one's opportunities and make the most of one's resources."*

— *Vauvenargues*

Grandpap understood that resources needed to be managed carefully and the knowledgeable leader also understands that this is one of the most important challenges he faces. Sometimes buying a well-marketed new resource may appear to be the solution to a problem but the ability to match the resource to the need is a valuable skill. Sometimes it appears that by saying yes to a new resource may be the easy road to keeping the staff happy but often those decisions come back to haunt you. Grandpap's barn was filled with old and new tools. He did not throw out those that may still be useful just because a new product was available.

A knowledgeable leader knows that he is in a position to request the resources he needs to run the organization. It is of no value for him to blame the policy makers or the level above him for the lack of resources. I have found it is a fine line that the leader must walk in supervising staff in their use of resources and giving them the understanding that does not tempt them to use limited resource as an excuse for their shortcomings.

An excellent solution is to give your employees choices from a menu of resources or tools that they would need. The decision of priorities became theirs but there could be no mistake that "all of the above" was a credible option just as was the plethora of tools available to me in Grandpap's barn.

## Lesson 16: Grandpap knew the importance of making decisions based on knowledge.

The sky was noticeably darker now, and it looked like the rain would find us before dinner. It occurred to Grandpap that he should begin to wrap up his work. He called over to me and we loaded the wheelbarrow with tools. "Bring the journal and yardstick with you from the shed," he said as I set off with the tools.

If there was one distinguishing characteristic that set Grandpap apart from other gardeners, it was the meticulousness with which he kept his data journals. In these notebooks, he charted a host of variables relevant to growing fruits and vegetables, including rainfall, daily temperature, plant size, and plant location, among others. In the winter months, he would use the data to evaluate the previous season's harvest and plan for the coming year.

## The knowledgeable leader understands the value of data-driven decisions in establishing trust and maintaining accountability.

*"We can't take credit for our talents. It's how we use them that counts."*

— *Madeline L'Engle*

*"Let us take things as we find them: let us not attempt to distort them into what they are not. We cannot make facts. All our wishing will not change them. We must use them."*

— *John Henry Cardinal Newman*

*"Get the facts, or the facts will get you. And when you get them, get them right, or they will get you wrong."*

— *Dr. Thomas Fuller*
*Gnomologia, 1732*

*"New knowledge is the most valuable commodity on earth. The more truth we have to work with, the richer we become."*

— *Kurt Vonnegut*
*Breakfast of Champions*

It is becoming more important to use data for decision making. Virtually every organization, whether it is non-profit or for-profit, must provide evidence of its performance to its governing board. Plans and priorities must be established after careful analysis of pertinent data. This is critical for both short term and long term decisions.

One of the most important tasks of a leader is to make judgments about which data to collect. Grandpap looked at his choice plants, the weather conditions, his gardening costs, his sales and kept records over several years. The leader must collect the data, examine it, look for patterns, interpret trends and determine strategies for responding to their findings.

When leaders ignore the data or let their egos and greed color their interpretations of data, outcomes are fragile and often disastorous. Data must be used with integrity and not manipulated. Lying with statistics has been the Achilles heel of many leaders and organizations.

Just as Grandpap understood how important knowledge was to making gardening decisions, data-driven decision making is essential in today's organizations. Stakeholders in all organizations are becoming more vocal concerning the decisions that cost money. It is absolutely essential for the knowledgeable leader to keep longitudinal records and, as was Grandpap's practice, it is important to use them to chart trends and plan for the future. The trust of the stakeholders of any organization is tenuous but the more accurate the records, the more likely the accountability issue will be addressed credibly.

# Lesson 17: Storms never appeared to be upsetting to Grandpap.

Just as soon as Grandpap began measuring the pepper plants, thunder erupted in the sky. Never rushing the data journals, he packed up and called to me. "Looks like watering time! Let's get the tools into the shed and head inside."

By the time we washed our hands and sat down inside, the storm was raging. Grandpap reviewed the day's journal entries and shared a few gains with me. He looked outside and pondered, "Nature waters the crops better than we can." "And less expensively," I added.

Although he had not finished his measurements, Pap sat there satisfied and proud. There would be time tomorrow to finish the work. He opened the newspaper and sank deeper into his chair.

## The effective leader must remain calm and poised in the face of adversity.

*"The ability to keep a cool head in an emergency, maintain poise in the midst of excitement, or refuse to be stampeded, are the true marks of leadership."*

— *R. Shannon*

*"No pessimist ever discovered the secrets of the stars, or sailed to an uncharted land, or opened a new heaven to the human spirit."*

— *Helen Keller*

*"Leadership is the ability to hide panic from others."*

— *Unknown*

*"Since we cannot change reality, let us change the eyes which see reality."*

— *Nikos Kazantzakis*

The effective leader recognizes that creative problem-solving can be a catalyst for change. Often when problems arise, it is the attitude of the leader that shapes its impact on the organization. Grandpap saw the storm as unavoidable and looked at the rain as an asset rather than an interruption.

Crises are often the impetus for change. Dr. A.J. Schuler analyzed the heroic manner in which Mayor Rudy Giuliani of the City of New York led his city after the terrorist attacks of September 11, 2001 in an article entitled, "Change Management Lessons of Rudy Giuliani, Post 9/11."[5] He concluded that Guilaini utilized the attacks as an opportunity for change in the city. Schuler summarized how Guiliani made those changes using five lessons. Change Management Lesson #1 is to articulate a positive vision for what you foresee as the future. Change Management Lesson #2: Be visible and calm, armed with critical information. Change Management Lesson #3: Raise the bar—challenge people to act out of a higher calling of service. Change Management Lesson #4: Set clear limits with compassion—and give people a clear choice ("iron hand in a velvet glove"). Change Management Lesson #5: Lavish public praise on those who choose to make positive contributions. Change Management Lesson #6: Don't cloud the message. By following these steps, Mayor Guiliani managed to take one of the world's most horrific crises and turn it into a revitalizing of the spirit of his city and our country's view of the importance and honor of our emergency services. By following his lessons, an effective leader may rise above the din of a crisis and discover an opportunity to reassess the organization in ways that can produce positive change.

The storms that threatened Mayor Guiliani and Grandpap could not have been more different, but their response to the storms were the same: calm and in control. Similarly, whatever storm threatens your organization should not be looked upon with panic but as an opportunity to adjust and grow from the experience.

[5](Dr. A. J. Schuler is an expert in leadership and organizational change. To find out more about his programs and services, visit www.SchulerSolutions.com or call (703) 370-6545.)

## Lesson 18: Always look forward to the annual county fair.

Grandpap was still reading the newspaper when dinner was served. "Look at this," he said, turning the paper toward Mom and me. "The County Fair is next month already!"

My memories of growing up in rural Southwestern Pennsylvania are filled with county fairs. We always had great luck selling our produce there, and Pap would give me half the day to explore the rides, games, and other food stands. Mom would make a special strawberry jam that was a hit every year. We even had a contest in the neighborhood to see who could grow the largest zucchini beforehand. The fair was a celebration of all we had worked for during the summer.

Pap said a blessing and we began to eat.

## The knowledgeable leader recognizes the value of external recognition of demonstrated success.

*"It's a funny thing about life; if you refuse to accept anything but the best, you very often get it."*
*— Somerset Maugham*

*"Always be a first-rate version of yourself, instead of a second-rate version of somebody else."*
*— Judy Garland*

*It's important that someone celebrate our existence . . . People are the only mirror we have to see ourselves in. The domain of all meaning. All virtue, all evil, are contained only in people. There is none in the universe at large. Solitary confinement is a punishment in every human culture.*
*— Lois McMaster Bujold,*
*Mirror Dance*

*"Recognition is the greatest motivator."*

*— Gerard C. Eakedale*

Celebrating success is important for all the stakeholders in an organization. As a leader, it is important to make those celebrations part of the culture. It is important that events are planned to bring all stakeholders together. Sometimes the opening of a new facility provides an opportunity for past successes and future dreams to be showcased. The anniversary of an organization's founding is another opportune time for celebration.

Applying for an award can be a rewarding experience for an organization because it requires the stakeholders to choose the best examples of their performance or product to compete. Just as was the case with the county fair, not everyone was chosen for an award. However, preparing for it had its own rewards.

Just as Grandpap selected the best examples of produce from his garden to exhibit, the knowledgeable leader understands that showcasing the best from his organization reaps great rewards. Whether this is done in a company brochure, a video production, a billboard or a portfolio for stockholders and stakeholders, the organization needs is strengthened by external recognition of success.

Seeing is believing. The greater investment of time, the greater the return on credibility of success. The knowledgeable leader understands and promotes this, recognizing that the value of the fair is not in the prizes; it is in the process that precedes the fair and the celebration of all who attend.

## CONCLUSION:

Now that you have read Grandpap's secrets to a great garden, I trust that you can see the quiet wisdom behind his lessons have a broad translation into the world around us. Keep in mind that Grandpap worked with passionate dedication to create his glorious garden. You must do the same for your organization if you want to experience success from his model. No two gardens are ever exactly alike and like those gardens the results you gain from Grandpap's tips may not be the same as another leader's results or even your own results from one year to the next. Your personality and vision must be incorporated into the lessons. Make the garden your own. I did and I can credit my grandpap for sharing with me the foundations for life that have allowed me to find happiness and success in both my family and professional life. Now that you too are equipped with Grandpap's wisdom, ask yourself this question:

How does your garden grow?

# References

Elbaz-Luwich, F. (1997) Narrative Research: Political Issues and Implications, Teaching and Teacher Education, 13(1) 75-83.

Friends Can Be Good Medicine,(1981) California Department of Health: Sacramento, California

Hatfield, John D. & Husseman, Richard C. (1989) The Equity Factor. Managing the Equity Factor. Houghton Mifflin: Boston, Massachusetts.

Hersey, Paul et.al (1993) Management of Organizational Behavior: Leading Human Resources (8th Edition) Prentice Hall: Upper Saddle River, New Jersey

Kofman, Fred & Senge, Peter M. (1995) "Communities of Commitment: The Heart of Learning Organizations," in Organizations: Developing Cultures for Tomorrow's Workplace, Productivity Press: Portland, Oregon

McClelland, David C. (1961) The Achieving Society, D. Van Nostrand Co., Inc.: Princeton, New Jersey.

Maslow, Abraham (1998) Maslow in Management, Wiley: New York, New York

Naisbitt, John (1994) Global Paradox, William Morrow & Co: New York, New York

Prelutsky, Jack (for Dr. Suess) (1998) Horray for Diffendoofer Day, Alfred A. Knopf: New York, New York

Sergiovanni, Thomas J. (1992) Moral Leadership: Getting to the Heart of School Leadership. Jossey-Bass: San Francisco, California

Printed in the United States
by Baker & Taylor Publisher Services